THE TRADITION

ALSO BY JERICHO BROWN

The New Testament

Please

JERICHO BROWN

THE TRADITION

CIVIC DIALOGUE EDITION

In collaboration with the On Being Project and the
Free Library of Philadelphia

COPPER CANYON PRESS
PORT TOWNSEND, WASHINGTON

Cover art: L. Ralphi Burgess, *You're in the Middle of the World*, ca. 2017,
acrylic and mixed media, 18" × 25"

Copper Canyon Press is in residence at Fort Worden State Park in Port
Townsend, Washington, under the auspices of Centrum. Centrum is a
gathering place for artists and creative thinkers from around the world,
students of all ages and backgrounds, and audiences seeking extraordinary
cultural enrichment.

LIBRARY OF CONGRESS CONTROL NUMBER
https://lccn.loc.gov/2022933171
Brown, Jericho, author. The Tradition : civic dialogue edition / Jericho
Brown, The On Being Project, Free Library of Philadelphia. Port Townsend :
Copper Canyon Press, 2022.
pages cm
ISBN: 9781556596421 (paperback)

98765432 FIRST PRINTING

COPPER CANYON PRESS
Post Office Box 271
Port Townsend, Washington 98368
www.coppercanyonpress.org

ACKNOWLEDGMENTS

Earlier versions of these poems appeared in the following journals and anthologies: The Academy of American Poets Poem-a-Day, *The American Poetry Review, The Baffler, Bennington Review, The Best American Poetry 2017, BOMB Magazine, Boston Review, BuzzFeed, The Georgia Review, The Golden Shovel Anthology: New Poems Honoring Gwendolyn Brooks, Gulf Coast, Memorious, The Nation, The New Criterion, The New Yorker, Opossum, Oxford American, The Paris Review, PEN Poetry Series, Phi Kappa Phi Forum, Poetry, Poetry London,* Poetry Society of America online, *The Rumpus, T: The New York Times Style Magazine, Time, Tin House, TriQuarterly, Vinyl,* and *Weber: The Contemporary West.*

This book was written with the support of the Bread Loaf Writers' Conference, Emory University, the John Simon Guggenheim Foundation, the Poetry Society of America, and the Sewanee Writers' Conference.

The supplemental materials included in *The Tradition: Civic Dialogue Edition* were developed in collaboration between Copper Canyon Press, the On Being Project, and the Free Library of Philadelphia. Copper Canyon Press extends special thanks to the compassionate and creative leaders of the On Being Project—Eddie Gonzalez, Lucas Johnson, Krista Tippet, and Pádraig Ó Tuama—and to the visionary and courageous team at the Free Library of Philadelphia—Tina Barber, Irma Qavolli, Ben Remsen, Brittanie Sterner, and Mariam Williams.

In memory of
Bertha Lee Lenoir
(1932–2018)

I will bring you a whole person
and you will bring me a whole person
and we will have us twice as much
of love and everything.

Mari Evans

CONTENTS

A NOTE FROM THE PUBLISHER

When *On Being*'s Krista Tippett interviewed Jericho Brown onstage at the 2018 Geraldine R. Dodge Poetry Festival—before *The Tradition* was published, before the Covid-19 pandemic changed every conversation and necessary outrage became more visible in the aftermath of George Floyd's murder—Jericho Brown was considering what we as a society of individuals might mean to one another. His poems were already living and sounding themselves into larger questions, creating conversations, prompting connection, and eliciting tears, joy, and desire for a civil society. He was anticipating the future, not merely mirroring the present, and in that interview he shared some of the poems from this book. The conversation that accompanied his appearance at the festival was enthralling and inspiring. (The transcript of that conversation is included later in this book and can be heard online at onbeing.org.)

After the publication of *The Tradition,* critical attention for the book grew rapidly, and award recognition quickly followed, culminating in the Pulitzer Prize for Poetry in 2020. The Pulitzer committee described *The Tradition* as "a collection of masterful lyrics that combine delicacy with historical urgency in their loving evocation of bodies vulnerable to hostility and violence."

Soon, at the height of the first wave of the pandemic, when every body was vulnerable, the Philadelphia Free Library decided to use *The Tradition* as part of a larger civic dialogue within the City of Philadelphia. *The Tradition* was the first book of poetry the library had ever brought into its One Book, One Philadelphia program, and through poetry they were creating a community conversation even as many of its patrons were living, reading, and loving in isolation. Copper Canyon Press was inspired and catalyzed by the library's work and the work of our colleagues at the On Being Project's *Poetry Unbound,* and we want to continue their empowering work through publication of *The Tradition, Civic Dialogue Edition.*

In the introduction to her discussion with Jericho, Krista Tippet quoted the director of the Dodge Poetry Festival, Martin Farawell:

> I think poetry evolved to save us from ourselves. It
> questions our understanding of what it means to be
> human and, in the process, deepens our humanity.
> History teaches us—and the daily news reminds
> us—how easily we forget what it means to be human.
> Probably no other art form is better than poetry at
> getting us directly inside another's mind, experience,
> perspective. The ability to imagine someone else's
> inner life is where compassion begins.

At Copper Canyon Press, we learned early on that *The Tradition* was a necessary and special book that spoke to a much larger community than we first imagined. We believe that this is a book that "deepens our humanity," and through the hard work and difficult questions of skilled facilitators this book can remind us of "what it means to be human." In this recognition—and with your help as a reader—we believe a conversation around these poems carries the potential to catalyze substantive change.

As Krista Tippett writes in *Poetry Unbound*'s "Better Conversations" guide:

> This is civic work and it is human, spiritual work—in
> the most expansive 21st-century sense of that lan-
> guage. We can learn for our time what moral imagi-
> nation, social healing, and civil discourse can look like

and how they work… And so it is up to us, where we live, to start having the conversations we want to be hearing and creating the realities we want to inhabit.

We invite you to read together, give voice to these poems, and allow the poems to give voice to those you gather with in community. In the following pages you will find guidance for conducting poetry reading groups and civic conversations about the world these poems make real.

COPPER CANYON PRESS

WINTER 2022

A NOTE FROM THE ON BEING PROJECT

You and I have it in us to be nourishers of discern-
ment, fermenters of healing. We have the language,
the tools, the virtues – and the calling, as human
beings – to create hospitable spaces for taking up the
hard questions of our time. This calling is too import-
ant and life-giving to wait for politics or media at their
worst to come around. We can discover how to calm
fear and plant the seeds of the robust civil society we
desire and that our age demands.

> —Krista Tippet, Founder and Editor
> in Chief

Carving out space to engage deeply with poetry and
quietly listen to what arises in ourselves in response
to what we've read is meaningful work. It involves
welcoming not only what we know and what feels set-
tled for us, but also what feels unsolved and uncertain,
complicated and even contradictory. Doing this inner
work, meeting ourselves anew with the possibility of
being surprised and even perplexed, we practice skills
that are important in engaging with others as well. We
can gain a greater awareness of our boundaries and
learning edges, grow comfortable with uncertainty,
and lean in with a spirit of generous curiosity that
seeks to understand ourselves and each other more
fully, increasing the chances that our conversations
might make the way for deepened relationship and
care, even across significant differences. This kind of
engagement is always available to us as an alternative

to practiced debates and polarized side-taking—a life-giving and healing move that looks to connect meaningfully and open up generative possibilities for shared life and vitality.

—Eddie Gonzalez, Director of
Engagement, Civil Conversations and
Social Healing

Rather than being directed by only one person, fruitful conversations can be guided by pop-up rules, as explored by Priya Parker in her *On Being* conversation with Krista, rules that help people gathered to agree on what will work for the purposes of their time together. Such rules are easily adaptable and are also a useful tool for a group turning attention toward the quality of their interaction. Again, the question of power arises: who gets to decide such temporary pop-up rules? To convene a conversation is to shape its borders, and any border can be hostile. Once again, the wisdom of our *On Being* conversation partners guides us: mediator John Paul Lederach suggests that unexpected gatherings of people, meeting in curiosity and care, can take risks in exploring how to create meaning in their time together. The way that such a group can help define its own pop-up rules can be the first topic of conversation. Taking care to listen to what is difficult to hear may be a way where unexamined privilege can learn to disarm itself.

—Pádraig Ó Tuama, Poet/Theologian
and Host of *Poetry Unbound*

Jericho Brown's beautiful work has offered us grounding for the conversations you will pursue. In this work, he's given us a window into life, and we have an opportunity to honor what he's shared with our questions, our curiosity, and our humility. Honoring that means to affirm the truth of people's experiences. Life is not something that any of us can interpret, comprehend, or live on our own. We need one another. There's no need to pretend otherwise. Most of us don't tell the stories of our lives, the stories of our pain in scientific, calculable ways. Poetry, when talking about the truth of our lives, or the truth of life, can sometimes make a lot more sense than prose. Listen for the poetry in the stories of those you plan to encounter. Listen for what's said and what's not said. Try not to crowd the air with words or thoughts that in the end don't matter but leave open hospitable space for what might arise in and between you.

      —Lucas Johnson, Executive Vice
        President, Public Life and Social Healing

A STARTER GUIDE

(Adapted from the On Being Project's *Poetry Unbound*, with assistance from the Philadelphia Free Library)

Any conversation begins before the conversation begins. Who decides the conversation should take place? Who issues the invitation? Who is the host? At On Being, we recognize that the host is as much a presence and power in the room as anyone, and there is no such thing as a neutral host. The practice of leadership is best guided by the truth that the role of leadership does not indicate access to all wisdom; leaders are often simply those who are willing to learn in public.

A conversation begins to unfold in the space that has been prepared, in the welcome one receives. We invite you to reflect on and use the guidance and ideas presented in the following pages as you engage in conversation about *The Tradition*.

Frame Your Guiding Intention

What questions would you like to pose and hold with others in the period ahead? This inquiry in itself is critical, and it deserves time, care, and cultivation. You might feel called to address a particular issue or challenge before your community. You might want to attend to nurturing courage and resilience for the life and work in which you and others are already engaged. You might feel called urgently to address different others in your community on a human level—humanizing the issues or putting them to one side while coming to know one another as people. And of course all of these longings and aims can find expression in the same process over time.

With the guidance of On Being, we are offering an adaptable framework to practice the virtues we've found to make new conversation and relationship possible, and to bring some collective wisdom from On Being, the Philadelphia Free Library, and Copper Canyon Press into your group as it forms the culture and spirit in which it will discern and act.

Grounding Virtues

What we practice, we become. These are the six grounding virtues that guide everything that the On Being Project does. Since On Being accomplishes extraordinary work in the world, we eagerly share them within *The Tradition: Civic Dialogue Edition*. As the folks at On Being remind us, virtues are not the stuff of saints and heroes. They are spiritual technologies and tools for the art of living.

WORDS THAT MATTER

We are starved for fresh language to approach one another. We need what Elizabeth Alexander calls "words that shimmer"—words with power that convey real truth, which cannot be captured in mere fact. Words have the force of action and become virtues in and of themselves.

The words we use shape how we understand ourselves, how we interpret the world, how we treat others. Words are one of our primary ways to reach across the mystery of each other. As technology reframes the meaning of basic human acts such as making and leading and belonging, the world needs the most vivid and transformative universe of words we can muster.

HOSPITALITY

Hospitality is a bridge to all the great virtues, but it is immediately accessible. You don't have to love or forgive or feel compassion to extend hospitality. But it's more than an invitation. It is the creation of an inviting, trustworthy space—an atmosphere as much as a place. It shapes the experience to follow. It creates the intention, the spirit, and the boundaries for what is possible. As creatures, it seems, we imagine a homogeneity in other groups that we know not to be there in our own. But new social realities are brought into being over time by a quality of relationship between unlikely combinations of people. When in doubt, practice hospitality.

HUMILITY

Humility is a companion to curiosity, surprise, and delight. Spiritual humility is not about getting small. It is about encouraging others to be big. It is not about debasing oneself but about approaching everything and everyone with a readiness to be surprised and delighted. This is the humility of the child. It is the humility in the spirituality of the scientist and the mystic—to be planted in what you know, while living expectantly for discoveries yet to come. The wisest people carry a humility that manifests as tenderness in a creative interplay with power.

PATIENCE

Like humility, patience is not to be mistaken for meekness and ineffectuality. It can be the fruit of a full-on reckoning with reality—a commitment to move through the world as it is, not as we wish it to be. A spiritual view of time is a long view of time—seasonal and cyclical, resistant to the illusion of time as a bully, time as a matter of deadlines. Human transformation takes time—longer than we want it to—but it is what is necessary for social transformation. A long, patient view of time will replenish our sense of our capacities and the hope we hold for the world.

GENEROUS LISTENING

Listening is an everyday art and virtue, but it's an art we have lost and must learn anew. Listening is more than being quiet while others have their say. It is about presence as much as receiving; it is about connection more than observing. Real listening is powered by curiosity. It involves vulnerability—a willingness to be surprised, to let go of assumptions and take in ambiguity. It is never in "gotcha" mode. The generous listener wants to understand the humanity behind the words of the other and patiently summons one's own best self and one's own most generous words and questions.

ADVENTUROUS CIVILITY

The adventure of civility for our time can't be a mere matter of politeness or niceness. Adventurous civility honors the difficulty of what we face and the complexity of what it means to be human. It doesn't celebrate diversity by putting it up on a pedestal and ignoring its messiness and its depths. The intimate and civilizational questions that perplex and divide us will not be resolved quickly. Civility, in our world of change, is about creating new possibilities for living forward while being different and even continuing to hold profound disagreement.

Shaping the Space

PLAN THE SPACE

Where will your gathering take place? What are the physical cues that will establish it as inviting and trustworthy? Take stock of how this works in familiar parts of life—what are the elements of hospitality when you entertain people you know and love? There might be food and drink. Think about the care you will give to entrances, seating, lighting, and welcoming. This will set the tone for everything that happens next.

WHO TO INVITE

There are many ways to think about who to invite, and they're all good. Is this a gathering of kindred spirits? A group to take up difficult issues at play in your community? A drawing in of people you want to know or be in conversation with but haven't known how to engage?

Decide who you know you want to be in the room. Then make a list of *bridge people* you'd love to reach out to—people of integrity who straddle kindred or disparate networks of interest to your own. Engage your core group of friends and community for ideas about intriguing bridge people out there and find someone who has a connection to extend a personal invitation. As you widen the circle, continue to bring to the surface the names of people your group would like to be in conversation with but haven't known how to meet. Include a generational mix. Invite someone younger whom you know to be interested and articulate and invite them to bring an interested friend, and invite at least one elder you know to be wise.

LAY THE GROUNDWORK

At least a week before the meeting, send a personal welcome letter. You might share the names of all who will be attending. Propose that everyone read the *The Tradition* and visit On Being's *Poetry Unbound* (https://onbeing.org/series/poetry-unbound/) before you meet as a springboard for discussion about the care and concerns you have for life in your community. Propose the possibility that some in the group might set aside time to listen together before you meet.

Gathering

SETTLING IN AND SETTING INTENTION

You might want to begin with a moment of silence. When you first meet, you could read all or part of the welcome letter aloud or ask someone else to do so. Emphasize in your letter that the point of this gathering, at least initially, is not to reach any resolution or conclusions. It is about creating and renewing common life. No one will be advocating to bring others to see things their way. No one will feel pressured to give up the ground they stand on. Stating this very clearly can be disarming, a relief for people. All of our favored cultural modes of engaging difference drive to resolution—winning the debate, getting on the same page, taking a vote. But there is value in learning to speak together honestly and relate to each other with dignity, without rushing to common ground that would leave all the hard questions hanging. We learn to speak differently together in order to live together differently.

PLANTING THE CONVERSATION

Every *On Being* interview begins with the question "Was there a spiritual or religious background to your childhood?" Everyone—everyone—has a great story to tell along these lines. But the real reason for starting with these kinds of questions is about where they plant the conversation—in a place in us that is softer and more searching than we usually present to the world. It's not a side of us that is usually invited into important discussions. Our answers are allowed to have questions attached, and our certainties are leavened by experiences, by hopes, and by fears. Reassure everyone that you have invited them to speak for themselves. No one is being asked to speak for their group, their position, their denomination or party, just for themselves. And insist on the confidentiality of what will happen. This is an essential practical part of creating a quiet, inviting, and trustworthy space—an environment, as Parker Palmer says, where the insights of the soul can come to the table.

Choose one of these questions and take it around the room. If you have a large gathering, you'll want to break up into smaller groups for this part, depending on size. Allow 5-10 minutes for each person depending on the group's size.

- Where do you trace the earliest roots of your passion for this conversation?

- Why are you here? What longing or curiosity made you say yes to this invitation?
- What hope and fear do you bring to this conversation?

DELVING

Kick off the discussion with your own reactions to the poems and materials in *The Tradition, Civic Dialogue Edition*. You might read a section that especially spoke to you, for those who may not have read all the materials themselves. Focus on these questions in your opening reflection, and invite them from others:

- What did I take from this?
- What challenged me?
- What felt relevant, helpful, or revealing of where we are as a community?

As the conversation gets going and others bring forth their thoughts and react to those of others, keep an ear open to helping people speak for themselves—not on behalf of a group and not lapsing into the jargon of issues and advocacy. This is how we've been trained to speak in groups, in public, and getting out of this mode takes some practice. But there is a profound difference between hearing someone say, "This is the truth," and hearing someone say, "This is my truth." You can disagree with another person's opinions, you can disagree with their doctrines, but you can't disagree with their experience.

- Can you tell me what you mean when you use that word?
- Would you put some bones on that idea for me?
- Can you tell a story to illustrate that?

CLOSING

In closing, formulate a question for everyone to carry out into the world and—if you plan to meet again—to frame your next gathering. You might get there by asking people to share one of the following:

- Something you've learned from someone else during the meeting.
- Something you're still thinking about.
- Something you want to talk more about at the next gathering.

Conversation Starters

Here are some questions you can use as conversation starters for gatherings that might take place over one or several sessions. Adapt them for your group and intentions, choosing questions you find meaningful or relevant.

When you first saw the title of the book, what was your response to the word "tradition"?

- What traditions do you see reflected in the book's title poem (p. 10)?
- Does the book expand your idea about what a "tradition" is or how it's formed?
- Are tradition and history the same?
- What is an example of a personal, familial, or national tradition you would like to break or to continue?

Choose a poem to read out loud.

- What do you notice when you read it aloud?
- Where do you find rhythmic sound or music in Jericho Brown's lines?
- What music or musical traditions does that remind you of?
- Where does that association take you?

"Blk is not a country, but I live there" ("After Avery R. Young," p. 22).

- How does this poem play with the idea of a country, of a place of belonging?

- Do you have parts of your identity that are not countries, but you feel like you "live there?"
- Do you live in more than one "country" or identity?
- When/where do you feel freest to be your whole self?

"We do not know the history / Of this nation in ourselves" ("Riddle," p. 28)

- After reading the poem, who do you think the "we" is?
- What is the difference between knowing history and knowing history "in ourselves"?
- In what ways do you know the history of our nation in yourself?

Read one of the "duplex" poems.

- How does Brown explore different ways humans experience memory—physically, emotionally, mentally, spiritually, and so on.
- How do recollections of pain and joy coexist in this duplex poem?
- How do you feel when you encounter a "duplex" within yourself?

THE TRADITION

Ganymede

A man trades his son for horses.
That's the version I prefer. I like
The safety of it, no one at fault,
Everyone rewarded. God gets
The boy. The boy becomes
Immortal. His father rides until
Grief sounds as good as the gallop
Of an animal born to carry those
Who patrol our inherited
Kingdom. When we look at myth
This way, nobody bothers saying
Rape. I mean, don't you want God
To want you? Don't you dream
Of someone with wings taking you
Up? And when the master comes
For our children, he smells
Like the men who own stables
In Heaven, that far terrain
Between Promise and Apology.
No one has to convince us.
The people of my country believe
We can't be hurt if we can be bought.

As a Human Being

There is the happiness you have
And the happiness you deserve.
They sit apart from each other
The way you and your mother
Sat on opposite ends of the sofa
After an ambulance came to take
Your father away. Some good
Doctor will stitch him up, and
Soon an aunt will arrive to drive
Your mother to the hospital
Where she will settle next to him
Forever, as promised. She holds
The arm of her seat as if she could
Fall, as if it is the only sturdy thing,
And it is, since you've done what
You always wanted, you fought
Your father and won, marred him.
He'll have a scar he can see all
Because of you. And your mother,
The only woman you ever cried for,
Must tend to it as a bride tends
To her vows, forsaking all others
No matter how sore the injury.
No matter how sore the injury
Has left you, you sit understanding
Yourself as a human being finally
Free now that nobody's got to love you.

Flower

Yellow bird.
Yellow house.
Little yellow
Song

Light in my
Jaundiced mouth.
These yellow
Teeth need

Brushing, but
You admire
My yellow
Smile. This

Black boy
Keeps singing.
Tiny life.
Yellow bile.

The Microscopes

Heavy and expensive, hard and black
With bits of chrome, they looked
Like baby cannons, the real children of war, and I
Hated them for that, for what our teacher said
They could do, and then I hated them
For what they did when we gave up
Stealing looks at one another's bodies
To press a left or right eye into the barrel and see
Our actual selves taken down to a cell
Then blown back up again, every atomic thing
About a piece of my coiled hair on one slide
Just as unimportant as anyone else's
Growing in that science
Class where I learned what little difference
God saw if God saw me. It was the start of one fear,
A puny one not much worth mentioning,
Narrow as the pencil tucked behind my ear, lost
When I reached for it
To stab someone I secretly loved: a bigger boy
Who'd advance
Through those tight, locker-lined corridors shoving
Without saying
Excuse me, more an insult than a battle. No large loss.
Not at all. Nothing necessary to study
Or recall. No fighting in the hall
On the way to an American history exam
I almost passed. Redcoats.
Red blood cells. Red-bricked
Education I rode the bus to get. I can't remember
The exact date or

Grade, but I know when I began ignoring slight alarms
That move others to charge or retreat. I'm a kind
Of camouflage. I never let on when scared
Of conflicts so old they seem to amount
To nothing really—dust particles left behind—
Like the viral geography of an occupied territory,
A region I imagine you imagine when you see
A white woman walking with a speck like me.

The Tradition

Aster. Nasturtium. Delphinium. We thought
Fingers in dirt meant it was our dirt, learning
Names in heat, in elements classical
Philosophers said could change us. *Stargazer.*
Foxglove. Summer seemed to bloom against the will
Of the sun, which news reports claimed flamed hotter
On this planet than when our dead fathers
Wiped sweat from their necks. *Cosmos. Baby's Breath.*
Men like me and my brothers filmed what we
Planted for proof we existed before
Too late, sped the video to see blossoms
Brought in seconds, colors you expect in poems
Where the world ends, everything cut down.
John Crawford. Eric Garner. Mike Brown.

Hero

She never knew one of us from another, so my brothers and I grew up
        fighting
Over our mother's mind
Like sun-colored suitors in a Greek myth. We were willing
To do evil. We kept chocolate around our mouths. The last of her
        mother's lot,
She cried at funerals, cried when she whipped me. She whipped me
Daily. I am most interested in people who declare gratitude
For their childhood beatings. None of them took what my mother gave,
Waking us for school with sharp slaps to our bare thighs.
That side of the family is darker. I should be grateful. So I will be—
No one on Earth knows how many abortions happened
Before a woman risked her freedom by giving that risk a name,
By taking it to breast. I don't know why I am alive now
That I still cannot impress the woman who whipped me
Into being. I turned my mother into a grandmother. She thanks me
By kissing my sons. Gratitude is black—
Black as a hero returning from war to a country that banked on his death.
Thank God. It can't get much darker than that.

After *Another Country*

Some dark of us dark,
The ones like me, walk
Around looking for
A building or a bridge.

We mumble and pull
At our lips, convinced,
Until we see how far
Down the distance.

We arrive to leave,
Calling ourselves
Cowards, but not you,
Rufus. You make it

To the George Washington—
Bold as an officer of the law
With the right to direct traffic
When all the stoplights

Are out—and you leap
Dirty against the whiteness
Of the sky to your escape
Through the whiteness

Of the water.

The Water Lilies

They open in the day and close at night.
They are good at appearances. They are white.
I judge them, judge the study they make
Of themselves, aspirational beings, fake
If you ask me. If you ask me, I'll say no,
Thank you, I don't need to watch what goes
Only imagining itself seen, don't need
To see them yawn their thin mouths and feed

On light, absolute and unmoved. They remind
Me of black people who see the movie
About slaves and exit saying how they would
Have fought to whip Legree with his own whip
And walked away from the plantation,
Their eyes raised to the sun, without going blind.

Foreday in the Morning

My mother grew morning glories that spilled onto the walkway
    toward her porch
Because she was a woman with land who showed as much by giving it
    color.
She told me I could have whatever I worked for. That means she was
    an American.
But she'd say it was because she believed
In God. I am ashamed of America
And confounded by God. I thank God for my citizenship in spite
Of the timer set on my life to write
These words: I love my mother. I love black women
Who plant flowers as sheepish as their sons. By the time the blooms
Unfurl themselves for a few hours of light, the women who tend them
Are already at work. Blue. I'll never know who started the lie that we
    are lazy,
But I'd love to wake that bastard up
At foreday in the morning, toss him in a truck, and drive him under
    God
Past every bus stop in America to see all those black folk
Waiting to go work for whatever they want. A house? A boy
To keep the lawn cut? Some color in the yard? My God, we leave
    things green.

The Card Tables

Stop playing. You do remember the card tables,
Slick stick figures like men with low-cut fades,
Short but standing straight
Because we bent them into weak display.
What didn't we want? What wouldn't we claim?
How perfectly each surface was made
For throwing or dropping or slamming a necessary
Portion of our pay.
And how could any of us get by
With one in the way?
Didn't that bare square ask to be played
On, beaten on the head, then folded, then put away,
All so we could call ourselves safe
Now that there was more room, a little more space?

Bullet Points

I will not shoot myself
In the head, and I will not shoot myself
In the back, and I will not hang myself
With a trashbag, and if I do,
I promise you, I will not do it
In a police car while handcuffed
Or in the jail cell of a town
I only know the name of
Because I have to drive through it
To get home. Yes, I may be at risk,
But I promise you, I trust the maggots
Who live beneath the floorboards
Of my house to do what they must
To any carcass more than I trust
An officer of the law of the land
To shut my eyes like a man
Of God might, or to cover me with a sheet
So clean my mother could have used it
To tuck me in. When I kill me, I will
Do it the same way most Americans do,
I promise you: cigarette smoke
Or a piece of meat on which I choke
Or so broke I freeze
In one of these winters we keep
Calling worst. I promise if you hear
Of me dead anywhere near
A cop, then that cop killed me. He took
Me from us and left my body, which is,
No matter what we've been taught,
Greater than the settlement

A city can pay a mother to stop crying,
And more beautiful than the new bullet
Fished from the folds of my brain.

Duplex

A poem is a gesture toward home.
It makes dark demands I call my own.

> Memory makes demands darker than my own:
> My last love drove a burgundy car.

My first love drove a burgundy car.
He was fast and awful, tall as my father.

> Steadfast and awful, my tall father
> Hit hard as a hailstorm. He'd leave marks.

Light rain hits easy but leaves its own mark
Like the sound of a mother weeping again.

> Like the sound of my mother weeping again,
> No sound beating ends where it began.

None of the beaten end up how we began.
A poem is a gesture toward home.

The Trees

In my front yard live three crape myrtles, *crying trees*
We once called them, not the shadiest but soothing
During a break from work in the heat, their cool sweat

Falling into us. I don't want to make more of it.
I'd like to let these spindly things be
Since my gift for transformation here proves

Useless now that I know everyone moves the same
Whether moving in tears or moving
To punch my face. A crape myrtle is

A crape myrtle. Three is a family. It is winter. They are bare.
It's not that I love them
Every day. It's that I love them anyway.

Second Language

You come with a little
Black string tied
Around your tongue,
Knotted to remind
Where you came from
And why you left
Behind photographs
Of people whose
Names now buck
Pronouncing. How
Do you say God
Now that the night
Rises sooner? Why
Must we wake to work
Before any alarm?
I am the man asking,
The great-grandson
Made so by the dead
Tenant farmers promised
A plot of woods to hew.
They thought they could
Own the dirt they were
Bound to. In that part
Of the country, a knot
Is something you get
After getting knocked
Down, and story means
Lie. In your plot
Of the country, class
Means school, this room

Where we practice
Words that undo your
Tongue when you tell
A lie or start a promise
Or unravel like a story.

After Avery R. Young

Blk is not a country, but I live there
Where even the youngest call you baby.
Sometimes you ain't we. Sometimes you is
Everybody. Washboard rains come. We
Open our mouths for a drink. Rather be radical
Than a fool. Oh and no,
We're not interested in killing
White people or making them
Work. Matter of truth, some snorted
Cocaine until folk started calling it
White lady. Slavery is a bad idea.
The more you look like me, the more we
Agree. Sometimes you is everybody.
The blk mind is a continuous
Mind. There is a we. I am among them.
I am one of the ones. I belong. Oom boom
Ba boom. I live there where
We have a right to expect something of the brother.
Hooking and crooking or punching the clock,
It's got to get done. That
Expectation. Stunning. Incantatory. Blk.
Power in our 24-hour
Barbershops. Power in the Stateville
Correctional Center. Power broke
Whether I have a car note or not.
Power under a quilt that won't unravel, though
I never met the woman who sewed it
Or the woman for whom it was a gift
Before it finally came to me. The blk mind
Is a continuous mind. I am not a narrative

Form, but dammit if I don't tell a story.
All land owned is land once stolen.
So the blues people of the world walk
On water. We will not die. Blk music.
Blk rage. Blk city of the soul
In a very cold town. Blk ice is ice you can't see.

A Young Man

We stand together on our block, me and my son,
Neighbors saying our face is the same, but I know
He's better than me: when other children move

Toward my daughter, he lurches like a brother
Meant to put them down. He is a bodyguard
On the playground. He won't turn apart from her,

Empties any enemy, leaves them flimsy, me
Confounded. I never fought for so much—
I calmed my daughter when I could cradle

My daughter; my son swaggers about her.
He won't have to heal a girl he won't let free.
They are so small. And I, still, am a young man.

In him lives my black anger made red.
They play. He is not yet incarcerated.

II

Duplex

The opposite of rape is understanding
A field of flowers called paintbrushes—

A field of flowers called paintbrushes,
Though the spring be less than actual.

Though the spring be less than actual,
Men roam shirtless as if none ever hurt me.

Men roam that myth. In truth, one hurt me.
I want to obliterate the flowered field,

To obliterate my need for the field
And raise a building above the grasses,

A building of prayer against the grasses,
My body a temple in disrepair.

My body is a temple in disrepair.
The opposite of rape is understanding.

Riddle

We do not recognize the body
Of Emmett Till. We do not know
The boy's name nor the sound
Of his mother wailing. We have
Never heard a mother wailing.
We do not know the history
Of this nation in ourselves. We
Do not know the history of our-
Selves on this planet because
We do not have to know what
We believe we own. We believe
We own your bodies but have no
Use for your tears. We destroy
The body that refuses use. We use
Maps we did not draw. We see
A sea so cross it. We see a moon
So land there. We love land so
Long as we can take it. Shhh. We
Can't take that sound. What is
A mother wailing? We do not
Recognize music until we can
Sell it. We sell what cannot be
Bought. We buy silence. Let us
Help you. How much does it cost
To hold your breath underwater?
Wait. Wait. What are we? What?
What on Earth are we? What?

Good White People

Not my phrase, I swear,
But my grandmother's
When someone surprised her
By holding open the door
Or by singing that same high C
Stephanie Mills holds
Near the end of "I Have Learned
To Respect the Power of Love"
Or by gifting her with a turkey
On the 24th of December
After a year of not tipping her
For cleaning what they could afford
Not to clean. You'll have to forgive
My grandmother with her *good*
Hair and her *good white people*
And her certified *good slap across*
Your mouth. Crack the beaten door
To eat or sing, but do not speak
Evil. Dead bad black woman
I still love, she didn't know
What we know. In America
Today, anyone can turn on
A TV or look out a window
To see several kinds of bird
In the air while each face watching
Smiles and spits, cusses and sings
A single anthem of blood—
All is stained. She was ugly.
I'm ugly. You're ugly too.
No such thing as good white people.

Correspondence

after *The Jerome Project* by Titus Kaphar
(oil, gold leaf, and tar on wood panels;
7" × 10½" each)

I am writing to you from the other side
Of my body where I have never been
Shot and no one's ever cut me.
I had to go back this far in order
To present myself as a whole being
You'd heed and believe in. You can trust me
When I am young. You can know more
When you move your hands over a child,
Swift and without the interruptions
We associate with penetration.
The young are hard for you
To kill. May be harder still to hear a kid cry
Without looking for a sweet
To slip into his mouth. Won't you hold him?
Won't you coo toward the years before my story
Is all the fault of our imaginations?
We can make me
Better if you like: write back. Or take the trip.
I've dressed my wounds with tar
And straightened a place for you
On the cold side of this twin bed.

Trojan

When a hurricane sends
Winds far enough north
To put our power out,
We only think of winning
The war bodies wage
To prove the border
Between them isn't real.
An act of God, so sweet.
No TV. No novel. No
Recreation but each
Other, and neither of us
Willing to kill. I don't care
That I don't love my lover.
Knowing where to stroke
In little light, knowing what
Will happen to me and how
Soon, these rank higher
Than a clear view
Of the face I'd otherwise
Flay had I some training
In combat, a blade, a few
Matches. Candles are
Romantic because
We understand shadows.
We recognize the shape
Of what once made us
Come, so we come
Thinking of approach
In ways that forgo
Substance. I'm breathing—

Heaving now—
In my own skin, and I
Know it. Romance is
An act. The perimeter
Stays intact. We make out
So little that I can't help
But imagine my safety.
I get to tell the truth
About what kind
Of a person lives and who
Dies. Barefoot survivors.
Damned heroes, each
Corpse lit on a pyre.
Patroclus died because
He could not see
What he really was inside
His lover's armor.

The Legend of *Big* and *Fine*

Long ago, we used two words
For the worth of a house, a car,
A woman—all the same to men
Who claimed them: things
To be entered, each to suffer
Wear and tear with time, but
Greater than the love for these
Was the strong little grin
One man offered another
Saying, *You lucky. You got you*
A big, fine _____.
Hard to imagine so many men
Waiting on each other to be
Recognized, every crooked
Tooth in our naming mouths
Ready like the syllables
Of a very short sentence, all
Of us crying *mine,* like babies who
Grab for what must be beautiful
Since someone else saw it.

The Peaches

I choose these two, bruised—
Maybe too ripe to take, fondling
As I toss them each
Into my cart, the smaller
With its stem somewhat
Intact—because they remind me
Of the girls who won't be girls
Much longer, both sealed
And secured like a monarch's
Treasure in a basement below
The basement of the house
I inherited. I've worked hard and want
To bring them something sweet
So they know I've missed them
More than anyone else. But first,
I weigh the peaches, pay
For them, make the short drive
To my childhood
Home of latches, mazes,
And locked doors. Every key
Mine now, though I've hidden a few
From myself. I pride myself
On my gifts. I can fashion for you
A place to play, and when you think
It's dark there, I hand you
Fruit like two swollen bulbs
Of light you can hold on to,
Watch your eyes brighten as you eat.

Night Shift

When I am touched, brushed, and measured, I think of myself
As a painting. The artist works no matter the lack of sleep. I am made
Beautiful. I never eat. I once bothered with a man who called me
Snack, Midnight Snack to be exact. I'd oblige because he hurt me
With a violence I mistook for desire. I'd get left hanging
In one room of his dim house while he swept or folded laundry.
When you've been worked on for so long, you never know
You're done. Paint dries. Midnight is many colors. Black and blue
Are only two. The man who tinted me best kept me looking a little
Like a chore. How do you say *prepared*
In French? How do you draw a man on the night shift? Security
At the museum for the blind, he eats to stay
Awake. He's so full, he never has to eat again. And the moon goes.

Shovel

I am not the man who put a bullet in its brain,
But I am commissioned to dispose of the corpse:
Lay furniture plastic next to it and roll it over
Until it is wrapped, tape with duct tape until
It is completely contained, lay next to that
Containment a tarp and roll it over until it is
Wrapped again, take cheap hardware twine
And tie it and tie it like a proper gift, a gift
A good child will give up on opening
Even come Christmas morning. I am here
To ignore the stench and throw the dead over
My left shoulder and carry it to the bed
Of a stolen truck. I did not steal the truck,
But there it is, outside the door, engine
Running. I do the driving and assume someone
Else must scrub the floors of the body's blood,
Scrub the body's last room of its evidence.
I do the driving and sing whatever love songs
The truck's radio affords me all the way
To the edge of anywhere hiking families refuse
To wander, and I dig and dig and dig as
Undertakers did before the advent of machinery,
Then lift, again, the dead, and throw, again,
The dead—quite tired now, winded really,
But my hands and shoulders and arms and legs
Unstoppable. I dump the body into the hole
I myself made, and I hum, some days, one
Of those love songs, some days, a song I myself
Make in my spinning head, which is wet
With sweat that drips into the hole I will not call

A grave. I sweat into the earth as I repair it.
I completely cover the dead before I return
The truck where I assume someone else must
Scrub it—engine off—of the body's evidence,
And I sing, again, those songs because I know
The value of sweet music when we need to pass
The time without wondering what rots beneath our feet.

The Long Way

Your grandfather was a murderer.
I'm glad he's dead.

He invented the toothbrush,
But I don't care to read his name

On the building I walk through

To avoid the rain. He raped women
Who weren't yet women.

I imagine the wealth he left
When you turn red. I imagine you as a baby

Bouncing on a rapist's knee. I like my teeth
Clean. I like to stay warm

And healthy. I get it. Then I get it
Again: my oral hygiene and your memory

Avoiding each other

Like a girl who walks the long way
To miss the neighborhood bully, like the bully

Who'd really rather beat up on somebody
New. I can't help you. I can't hug you.

I can't grip your right hand, though
It never held a gun, though it never

Covered a lovely mouth, and you can't pay me
To cross the ground floor without wishing

I could spit on or mar some slick surface

And not think of who will have to do the cleaning.
We'd all still be poor. I'd end up drenched

Going around. You'd end remembering
What won't lead to a smile that gleams

In dark places. Some don't know
How dark. Some do.

Dear Whiteness

Come, love, come lie down, love, with me
In this king-size bed where we go numb
For each other letting sleep take us into
Ease, a slumber made only when I hold
You or you hold me so close I have no idea
Where I begin—where do you end?—where you

Tell me lies. Tell me sweet little lies

About what I mean to you when
I've labored all day and wish to come
Home like a war hero who lost an arm.
That's how I fight to win you, to gain
Ground you are welcome to divide
And name. See how this mouth opens
To speak what language you allow me
With the threat of my head cradled safe.

Tell me lies. Tell me sweet little lies

Of what you require, intimacy so industrious
That when I wake to brush you from my own
Teeth I see you in the mirror. I won't stay
Too long. When you look in that mirror, it
Will be clean. You'll be content
Seeing only yourself. Was I ever there?

Tell me lies. Tell me. Tell me lies.

Of the Swan

The luck of it: my ordinary body
Once under

A god. No night ends his
Care, how

He finishes a fixed field, how he
Hollows

A low tunnel. He released me
After. Why

Else pray like a woman
Ruined

By an ever-bitter extremity?
Men die,

But God's soul rises out of its black
Noose, finds

Bared skin a landscape prepared
For use—

Immortality requires worship.
I was

The Lord's opening on Earth,
A woman

With feathers strewn round
My hide.

Entertainment Industry

Scared to see a movie
All the way through
       I got to scream each scene
       Duck and get down
       Mass shooting blues

When you see me coming
You see me running
When you see me running
You run too

I don't have kids
Cuz I'd have to send them to school
       Ain't that safe as any
       Plan for parenthood
       Mass shooting blues

When you see me coming
You see me running
If you can beat a bullet
You oughta run too

Stake

I am a they in most of America.
Someone feels lost in the forest
Of we, so he can't imagine
A single tree. He can't bear it.
A cross. A crucifixion. Such
A Christian. All that wood
Headed his way in the fact
Of a man or a woman who
Might as well be a secret, so
Serious his need to see inside.
To cut down. To tell. How
Old will I get to be in a nation
That believes we can grow out
Of a grave? Can reach. Climb
High as the First State Bank.
Take a bullet. Break through
Concrete. The sidewalk.
The street someone crosses
When he sees wilderness where
He wanted his city. His cross-
Tie. His telephone pole.
Timber. Timbre. It's an awful
Sound, and people pay to hear
It. People say bad things about
Me, though they don't know
My name. I have a name.
A stake. I settle. Dig. Die.
Go underground. Tunnel
The ocean floor. Root. Shoot
Up like a thought someone
Planted. Someone planted

An idea of me. A lie. A lawn
Jockey. The myth of a wooded
Hamlet in America, a thicket,
Hell, a patch of sunlit grass
Where any one of us bursts into
One someone as whole as we.

Layover

Dallas is so
Far away
Even for the people
Who live
In Dallas a hub
Through which we get
To smaller places
That lurch
And hurt going
Home means stopping
In Dallas and all are
From little
Towns and farms
If all keep
Heading back
Far enough pay
Attention keep
Your belongings
Near everyone
In Dallas is
Still driving
At 3:24 a.m.
Off I-20 where
I was raped
Though no one
Would call it
That he was
Hovering by
The time
I understood

He thought it necessary
To leave me with knowledge
I can be
Hated I was
Smaller then
One road went
Through me
No airport
I drove
Him home
A wreck
On the freeway
We sat
In traffic
My wallet
On the seat
In between
My legs

III

Duplex

I begin with love, hoping to end there.
I don't want to leave a messy corpse.

      I don't want to leave a messy corpse
      Full of medicines that turn in the sun.

Some of my medicines turn in the sun.
Some of us don't need hell to be good.

      Those who need most, need hell to be good.
      What are the symptoms of *your* sickness?

Here is one symptom of my sickness:
Men who love me are men who miss me.

      Men who leave me are men who miss me
      In the dream where I am an island.

In the dream where I am an island,
I grow green with hope. I'd like to end there.

Of My Fury

I love a man I know could die
And not by way of illness
And not by his own hand
But because of the color of that hand and all
His flawless skin. One joy in it is
Understanding he can hurt me
But won't. I thought by now I'd be unhappy
Unconscious next to the same lover
So many nights in a row. He readies
For bed right on the other side
Of my fury, but first, I make a braid of us.
I don't sleep until I get what I want.

After Essex Hemphill

The night is the night. So
Say the stars that light us
As we kneel illegal and
Illegal like Malcolm X.
This is his park, this part
Of the capital where we
Say please with our mouths
Full of each other, no one
Hungry as me against this
Tree. This tree, if we push
Too hard, will fall. But if
I don't push at all, call me
A sissy. Somebody ahead
Of me seeded the fruit-
Bearing forest. The night
Is my right. Shouldn't I
Eat? Shouldn't I repeat,
It was good, like God?

Stay

It was restful, learning nothing necessary.

Gwendolyn Brooks

All day, I kept still just to think of it—

Your body above mine, what was
A lack of air between us—hot but restful

As I sat center on my bed of learning,

Mouth open, touching nothing,
My memory the only noise necessary.

A.D.

Each wounds you badly, but no boy hurts
Like the first one

                When you slept in a bed
Too narrow for two. You thought he disappeared

             In the sheet and cushion,
But look at you now, twenty-eight in a king, you wake

With a man on your mind— Head
On your chest, both of you bent

As best you can to make
Room for the other.

Ten years, your feet hanging, tangled and long, and still
You're the victim

Of such nightmares. You breathe
Like he's been lying

              On top for the last decade.
A man goes to heaven, you suffocate below the weight.

Turn You Over

All my anxiety is separation anxiety.
I want to believe you are here with me,
But the bed is bigger and the trash
Overflows. Someone righteous should
Take out my garbage. I am so many odd
And enviable things. Righteous is not
One of them. I'd rather a man to avoid
Than a man to imagine in a realm
Unseen, though even the doctor who
Shut your eyes swears you're somewhere
As close as breath. Mine, not yours.
You don't have breath. You got
Heaven. That's supposed to be my
Haven. I want you to tell me it sparkles
There. I want you to tell me anything
Again and again while I turn you over
To quiet you or to wake and remind you
I can't be expected to clean up after a man.

The Virus

Dubbed undetectable, I can't kill
The people you touch, and I can't
Blur your view
Of the pansies you've planted
Outside the window, meaning
I can't kill the pansies, but I want to.
I want them dying, and I want
To do the killing. I want you
To heed that I'm still here
Just beneath your skin and in
Each organ
The way anger dwells in a man
Who studies the history of his nation.
If I can't leave you
Dead, I'll have
You vexed. Look. Look
Again: show me the color
Of your flowers now.

The Rabbits

I caught them
In couples on the lawn
As I pulled into my driveway
After a night of bare music,
Of drinking on my feet
Because I think I look better
Standing. I should lie. Say
They expressed my desire
To mount and be
Mounted as they scurried
Into the darkest parts of what
I pay for, but I am tired
Of claiming beauty where
There is only truth: the rabbits
Heard me coming and said
Danger in whatever tongue
Stops them from making
More. I should say
I understood myself
That way, as danger, engine
Idling, but I thought
Infestation. Now I worry
No one will ever love me—
Furry little delights fucking
In my own front yard and I,
I am reminded of all I've gotten
Rid of. And every living
Thing that still must go.

Monotheism

Some people need religion. Me?
I've got my long black hair. I twist
The roots and braid it tight. *You're*

My villain. You're a hard father, from
Behind, it whines, tied and tucked,
Untouchable. Then comes

The night— Before I carry my
Mane to bed with me, I sit us
In front of the vanity. Undo. Un-

Wind. *Finally your fingers,* it says
Near my ear, *Your fingers. Your
Whole hands. No one's but yours.*

Token

Burg, boro, ville, and wood,
I hate those tiny towns,
Their obligations. If I needed
Anyone to look at me, I'd dye my hair purple
And live in Bemidji. Look at me. I want to dye
My hair purple and never notice
You notice. I want the scandal
In my bedroom but not in the mouths of convenience
Store customers off the nearest highway. Let me be
Another invisible,
Used and forgotten and left
To whatever narrow miseries I make for myself
Without anybody asking
What's wrong. Concern for my soul offends me, so
I live in the city, the very shape of it
Winding like the mazes of the adult-video outlets
I roamed in my twenties: pay a token to walk through
Tunnels of men, quick and colorless there where we
Each knew what we were,
There where I wasn't the only one.

The Hammers

They sat on the dresser like anything
I put in my pocket before leaving
The house. I even saw a few little ones
Tilted against the window of my living
Room, metal threats with splinters
For handles. They leaned like those
Teenage boys at the corner who might
Not be teenage boys because they ask
For dollars in the middle of the early
April day and because they knock
At 10 a.m. Do I need help lifting some-
Thing heavy? Yard work? The boys
Seemed not to care that they lay
On the floor lit by the TV. I'd have
Covered them up with linen, with dry
Towels and old coats, but their claw
And sledge and ball-peen heads shone
In the dark, which is, at least, a view
In the dark. And their handles meant
My hands, striking surfaces, getting
Shelves up, finally. One hung
From the narrow end of a spoke
In the ceiling fan, in wait of summer.
I found another propped near the bulb
In the refrigerator. Wasn't I hungry?
Why have them there if I could not
Use them, if I could not look at my own
Reflection in the mirror and take one
To the temple and knock myself out?

I Know What I Love

It comes from the earth.
It is green with deceit.
Sometimes what I love
Shows up at three
In the morning and
Rushes in to turn me
Upside down. Some-
Times what I love just
Doesn't show up at all.
It can hurt me if it
Means to… because
That's what *in love*
Means. What I love
Understands itself
As properly scarce.
It knows I can't need
What I don't go without.
Some nights I hold
My breath. I turn as in
Go bad. When I die
A man or a woman will
Clean up the mess
A body makes. They'll
Talk about gas prices
And the current drought
As they prepare the blue-
Black cadaver that still,
As the dead do, groans:
I wanted what anyone
With an ear wants—
To be touched and

Touched by a presence
That has no hands.

Crossing

The water is one thing, and one thing for miles.
The water is one thing, making this bridge
Built over the water another. Walk it
Early, walk it back when the day goes dim, everyone
Rising just to find a way toward rest again.
We work, start on one side of the day
Like a planet's only sun, our eyes straight
Until the flame sinks. The flame sinks. Thank God
I'm different. I've figured and counted. I'm not crossing
To cross back. I'm set
On something vast. It reaches
Long as the sea. I'm more than a conqueror, bigger
Than bravery. I don't march. I'm the one who leaps.

Deliverance

Though I have not shined shoes for it,
Have not suffocated myself handsome
In a tight, bright tie, Sunday comes
To me again as it did in childhood.

We few left who listen to the radio leave
Ourselves available to surprise. We pray
Unaware of prayer. We are an ugly people.

Forgive me, I do not wish to sing
Like Tramaine Hawkins, but Lord if I could
Become the note she belts halfway into
The fifth minute of "The Potter's House"

When black vocabulary heralds home-
Made belief: *For any kind of havoc, there is
Deliverance!* She means that even after I am

Not listening. I am not a saint
Because I keep trying to be a sound, something
You will remember
Once you've lived enough not to believe in heaven.

Meditations at the New Orleans Jazz
National Historical Park

1

Dear Tom Dent,
We still love you
And love what
It means to be
A black college
President's son
Whose pride
And rebellion
Look like men
In the Seventh Ward.
They groaned
For you, and
Ain't that music
Too, bodies
Of several
Shades arranged
For one sound
Of want or
Without or *wish*
A Negro would— Come
Back home,
Little light
Skin, come
Give Daddy
A kiss.

2

I present myself that you might

Understand how you got here
And who you owe. As long as

I can remember the brass band, it
Lives, every goodbye a lie. Every
One of them carries the weight

He chose. And plays it. No theft.
No rape. No flood. No. Not in
This moment. Not in this lovely

Sunlit room of my mind. Holy.

So the Bible says, in the beginning,
Blackness. I am alive. You?
Alive. You born with the nerve

To arrive yawning. You who
Walk without noticing your feet
On an early morning swept hard-

Wood floor: because Eve, because
Lucy. The whole toe of my boot,

Tapping.

3

This chair
Is where
I understand
I am
Nothing if
I can't
Sit awhile
In the audience
Or alone, sit
Down awhile
And thank God
The seat
Has stayed
Warm.

Dark

I am sick of your sadness,
Jericho Brown, your blackness,
Your books. Sick of you
Laying me down
So I forget how sick
I am. I'm sick of your good looks,
Your debates, your concern, your
Determination to keep your butt
Plump, the little money you earn.
I'm sick of you saying no when yes is as easy
As a young man, bored with you
Saying yes to every request
Though you're as tired as anyone else yet
Consumed with a single
Diagnosis of health. I'm sick
Of your hurting. I see that
You're blue. You may be ugly,
But that ain't new.
Everyone you know is
Just as cracked. Everyone you love is
As dark, or at least as black.

Duplex

Don't accuse me of sleeping with your man
When I didn't know you had a man.

     Back when I didn't know you had a man,
     The moon glowed above the city's blackout.

I walked home by moonlight through the blackout.
I was too young to be reasonable.

     He was so young, so unreasonable,
     He dipped weed in embalming fluid.

He'd dip our weed in embalming fluid.
We'd make love on trains and in dressing rooms.

     Love in the subway, love in mall restrooms.
     A bore at home, he transformed in the city.

What's yours at home is a wolf in my city.
You can't accuse me of sleeping with a man.

Thighs and Ass

Where I am my thickest, I grew
Myself by squat and lunge, and all

The time I sweated, I did not think
        Of being divided or entered, though

Yes, I knew meat would lure men,
        And flesh properly placed will lead

        One to think that he can—when
He runs from what sniffs to kill us—

Mount my back trusting I may carry
        Him at a good speed for a long distance,

        And to believe, believe that
When he hungers, I am able

To leap high, snatch
        The fruit of the tree

We pause to hide behind and feed, feed him.

Cakewalk

My man swears his HIV is better than mine, that his has in it a little gold, something he can spend if he ever gets old, claims mine is full of lead: slows you down, he tells me, looking over his shoulder. But I keep my eyes on his behind, say my HIV is just fine. Practical. Like pennies. Like copper. It can conduct electricity. Keep the heat on or shock you. It works hard, earns as much as my smile.

Stand

Peace on this planet
Or guns glowing hot,
We lay there together
As if we were getting
Something done. It
Felt like planting
A garden or planning
A meal for a people
Who still need feeding,
All that touching or
Barely touching, not
Saying much, not adding
Anything. The cushion
Of it, the skin and
Occasional sigh, all
Seemed like work worth
Mastering. I'm sure
Somebody died while
We made love. Some-
Body killed somebody
Black. I thought then
Of holding you
As a political act. I
May as well have
Held myself. We didn't
Stand for one thought,
Didn't do a damn thing,
And though you left
Me, I'm glad we didn't.

Duplex: Cento

My last love drove a burgundy car,
Color of a rash, a symptom of sickness.

   We were the symptoms, the road our sickness:
   None of our fights ended where they began.

None of the beaten end where they begin.
Any man in love can cause a messy corpse,

   But I didn't want to leave a messy corpse
   Obliterated in some lilied field,

Stench obliterating lilies of the field,
The murderer, young and unreasonable.

   He was so young, so unreasonable,
   Steadfast and awful, tall as my father.

Steadfast and awful, my tall father
Was my first love. He drove a burgundy car.

NOTES

The italicized portion of "After Avery R. Young" is a 2010 quotation from Louis Farrakhan, the leader of the Nation of Islam (which has its headquarters in Chicago, Illinois).

The italicized lines in "Dear Whiteness" are from "Little Lies" by Fleetwood Mac from the album *Tango in the Night* (Warner Bros. Records, 1987).

"Duplex (I begin with...)" is for L. Lamar Wilson.

"The Hammers" is modeled after "What the Angels Left" by Marie Howe.

JERICHO BROWN: SMALL TRUTHS
AND OTHER SURPRISES

Transcript of *On Being* interview with Krista Tippet, October 1, 2020

The poet Jericho Brown reminds us to bear witness to the complexity of the human experience, to interrogate the proximity of violence to love, and to look and listen closer so that we might uncover the small truths and surprises in life. His presence is irreverent and magnetic, as the high school students who joined us for this conversation experienced firsthand at the 2018 Geraldine R. Dodge Poetry Festival. And now he's won the 2020 Pulitzer Prize for Poetry.

KRISTA TIPPETT, HOST: Jericho Brown is beloved in the worlds of poetry and education. And now the book he was writing when we spoke, *The Tradition*, has won the 2020 Pulitzer Prize for Poetry. We had an audience of Newark high school students for this conversation — ranging from the proximity of violence and love, the complexity each of us is, and small truths and the surprises they bring. Plus it was fun to read Jericho's own words back to him.

[*music: "Seven League Boots" by Zoë Keating*]

TIPPETT: "Only the creative mind can make use of hope. Only a creative people can wield it."

JERICHO BROWN: Come on, creative people. I got some creative people out there, yes, God.

[*applause* and *laughter*]

TIPPETT: I'm Krista Tippett, and this is *On Being*.

Jericho Brown is associate professor and the director of the creative writing program at Emory University. We recorded our conversation onstage at the 2018 Geraldine R. Dodge Festival — where we were introduced by the Dodge Foundation's program director, Martin Farawell.

[*applause*]

TIPPETT: So here's some of what Martin first wrote to us in the invitation he sent to be part of this. He said, "I think poetry evolved to save us from ourselves. It questions our understanding of what it means to be human and, in the process, deepens our humanity. History teaches us — and the daily news reminds us — how easily we forget what it means to be human. Probably no other art form is better than poetry at getting us directly inside another's mind, experience, perspective. The ability to imagine someone else's inner life is where compassion begins." And he said, "We could certainly use more of that nowadays." Amen. [*laughs*]

I am also personally grateful for this invitation because it has introduced me to Jericho Brown — to his person and his poetry. I have some poems that I've marked, but if you, in the course of the next hour, just feel called to stand up and read a particular poem, you are warmly invited to do so.

BROWN: Do I have to stand up?

TIPPETT: No, you can sit. [*laughs*]

You grew up in Shreveport, Louisiana? I begin many of my conversations with a question about the religious or spiritual background of someone's early life, their childhood, and also the origins of the passions and questions that drive them. And it seemed to me, as I started exploring you, that some of the convergence of your story of growing up in church, in the Black Baptist Church, and also, what

78

becoming a poet meant to you — some of that story is wrapped up in the name you chose as an adult, that Jericho is not the name you were born with.

I wonder if you would reflect on that. Do you think that's true, to say that those things come together in your name?

BROWN: Maybe so. I think one thing that I love about being a poet is that I know that I was prepared for it in every way possible, and one of the ways that I was prepared for it is growing up in a black church. And when I say "growing up in a black church," I mean, people really went all the way toward pageantry and toward drama and toward what they were going to wear. Everything they could possibly give it, they gave to being in that moment. And the energy in that church, the energy in that sanctuary, was always high, and everyone was aware that they were doing it, that the energy was high energy because we were making it high energy with our song, with the way we spoke, with the way we moved. Many of you have been to churches, and you know that when you go to a black church, there is no — "Hello" is "Hello! And how are you this morning?" Everything was so grand. And a song where the note is "ahh" turns into "aaahaaahaaahaaah." It's always a little something more, where everything is being given an individual life — "This is what my individual self is bringing to it."

And when I changed my name, I didn't really think about it in a religious way, although obviously the name is biblical. It's a city that is biblical ...

TIPPETT: Yeah, I wondered what that summoned up for you.

BROWN: But I was thinking about something that I do associate with the church — I was thinking about, the other night, how I never had this problem where — people have this problem where they're afraid to write about their family. But I always understood

that in my poems, if I were to be writing about the father, because
of the subject matter of my poems, if I say "father," I'm not just
talking about my dad. I'm also talking about that father, God, that
I was taught in church. And if I say "father," that also would have
resonance with "fatherland" and "motherland," thinking about
America, thinking about the continent of Africa that is unknown to
me in so many ways and yet a part of me, culturally. And so when I
first started publishing my poems, they came under the name Nelson
Demery III. Can y'all believe that?

[*laughter*]

TIPPETT: And your father was Nelson Demery II?

BROWN: "Jr.," not "II." And my grandfather was "Senior." And
when I would see my poems come out, they didn't feel like they
were — I wanted them to be mine. And so, me changing my name
had a lot to do with, like I was saying, trying to be the individual
that emerges within the community.

TIPPETT: Do I understand it correctly, also, that you changed your
name when you started writing, really pouring yourself more deeply
into sensitive things like your relationship with your father, your
earthly father, and also with being gay and how those things came
together?

BROWN: Well, when I was first writing, I wanted more than any-
thing to be able to give all of myself to my poems. And I don't
know if I would think that I had to do this now, but at the time, I
really believed I had to completely transform in order to do that.
Adrienne Rich talks about this in "When We Dead Awaken: Writing
as Re-Vision," one of my favorite essays. Please read it if you hav-
en't. Langston Hughes talks about this in "The Negro Artist and
the Racial Mountain." T. S. Eliot talks about this in "Tradition and
the Individual Talent." It's this idea that whatever we're writing,

we have to be free. You have to have, at your access, in the midst of writing, all of your memories, all of your knowledge, all of your beliefs. And all of those things could get turned on their head — that what you thought was most valuable comes into question, and you have to be willing to go there while you're writing a poem.

It's a very dangerous place to be. It's the reason why, if I'm on an airplane and somebody asks me what I do for a living, I very quickly tell them I'm a poet. Then I don't have to worry about them talking to me anymore.

[*laughter*]

Do you know what I'm saying? Because people intuitively or instinctively, people know, "Oh, you're dangerous. You're hugely problematic. You're asking yourself questions that I've been avoiding my whole life, and you think that's a good time." Do you understand what I'm saying?

So, me giving myself that name was a way for me to become somebody who wasn't connected to anything that would say to me that I shouldn't be doing what I was doing. And I needed to be who I am now. I needed to be Jericho Brown, because I needed to have that freedom named. And that's what I was to call that freedom, was Jericho.

TIPPETT: There's a poem called "Our Father."

BROWN: "Like Father."

TIPPETT: "Like Father."

BROWN: Yeah, yeah, yeah. I wrote it.

TIPPETT: OK, there was me, transposing my Baptist childhood onto the title of the poem.

BROWN: I know; that's what happens.

TIPPETT: Would you read that one?

BROWN: Yeah, I'll read it.

Like Father

"My father's embrace is tighter
Now that he knows
He is not the only man in my life.
He whispers, *Remember when*, and, *I love you*,
As he holds my hand hungry
For a discussion of Bible scriptures
Over breakfast. He pours cups of coffee
I can't stop
Spilling.
My father's embrace is firm and warm
Now that he knows. He begs forgiveness
For anything he may have done to make me
Turn to abomination
As he watches my eggs, scrambled
Soft. Yolk runs all over the plate.
A rubber band binds the morning paper.
My father's embrace tightens. Grits
Stiffen. I hug back
Like a little boy, gripping
To prove his handshake.
Daddy squeezes me close,
But I cannot feel his heartbeat
And he cannot hear mine —
There is too much flesh between us,
Two men in love."

[*applause*]

TIPPETT: I feel like something that you reveal and work with in your poetry — and it was certainly in that — somewhere, I don't know whose phrase this was, but "where tenderness meets violence" and where love meets alienation, and yet, they're both in the same room at the same time — and in the same bodies and in the same bodies touching.

BROWN: Well, all of my work seems to go back to this place where love and brutality somehow come together. And when I say that, people are like, "No, they don't. Love and brutality don't come together."

TIPPETT: Not in the abstract.

BROWN: But all you got to do is have kids or a parent, and you actually do know what it's like to feel like "Oh, I could actually kill you …" [*laughs*] " … but I'm not, 'cause I love you." Do you know what I mean?

We put ourselves through huge inconveniences that are like certain kinds of violence, when we fall in love. Is there somebody in this room who's driven from Massachusetts to California to see somebody for two days? I'm willing to — I know somebody in this room has done that. Do you know what I mean? So I'm interested in where love goes awry or where people use violence as an excuse for love. And I'm interested in seeing how that comes out in my poems, because it's where I can keep asking myself questions. It's something that I don't understand. And I think poems are better built out of what we don't understand, not what we do already know, but what we're trying to figure out and better understand.

TIPPETT: That's an interesting way to say it. And they let what we don't understand — they let that be in the room. They let that be real. And they don't contain that urgency when — the ways we converse and discuss and are in dialogue beyond poetry, there's this compulsion to solve it or to simplify it. Or, then, if we can't do either one of those things, to move away. Poetry lets you stay present to that — with the discomfort, but also with the mystery of it.

BROWN: It's part of actually what we're doing — this is part of why people have a hard time with meditation, because to truly be in the mode of meditation, you can't have judgment on a thought. You just look at the thought. You can't have judgment on a pain in the body. You just look at the pain in the body, and you register things without saying, "Oh, this is good" or "This is bad." It just is.

And then I think you come away from that thinking, "Oh, well, it must be good, because here I still am." Do you know what I mean?

TIPPETT: Or, and also, "I can survive this."

BROWN: Yeah. Poems have to make our lives clear. Poems have to make our lives real on the page. And nobody's living an easy life. Nobody's living a life that is anything other than complex. And there are things about our lives that TV's not going to give us, that movies, even, are not going to give us. And poems are where I go for that. That's where I go for the complexity, the thing in us that we don't really understand. 'Why would you act like that? Why would you say that thing? How could you commit that evil?'

Every murderer's got a mama. But we don't like to think about that. But that's true; they came from somewhere. So that's the kind of thing I'm interested in.

TIPPETT: I feel like you are a natural-born conversationalist. I said this to you backstage — you're easy; I'm not worried about this. [*laughs*]

BROWN: I hope so.

TIPPETT: I feel like — when I was getting ready to interview you, and I was looking at other interviews you'd given, and I felt like we could just sit down out here, and I could say, "Hi…"

BROWN: Hey.

TIPPETT: … and then we could go for an hour.

BROWN: I'm for it.

TIPPETT: And you were also a speechwriter for the mayor of New Orleans, is that right? So I was trying to figure out, how do I focus this? And I found this interview you did in the *Kenyon Review*. Do you remember this? And they had asked you at the end — they wanted to talk about what would your credo be; what core beliefs do you have about literature and books. And you gave — it was a beautiful, beautiful answer.

And I just want to pull a couple of those out, and this very much follows on what you were just saying, although the word you didn't use is, we haven't mentioned the word "politics" now. And here's something you said: "Every poem is a love poem. Every poem is a political poem, so say the masters. Every love poem is political. Every political poem must fall in love." You also said, "You can't love me if you don't love politically." So tell us.

BROWN: [*laughs*] Tell you how to love me?

TIPPETT: [*laughs*] No, tell us — take us inside this very big thought.

BROWN: No, just — I think — I'm interested in all of people. And there's something in us that wants to really take people down to some sort of census report, I guess; and I'm not interested in census reports. I'm interested in how you got here today and how you managed to do your makeup in the car in order to do it. I'm interested in that. I'm interested in the fact that you got two kids, and you're getting married, and now you're pregnant, and you're going to have another kid, and you're trying to figure out how these kids are all going to call each other sister and brother.

I'm interested in that. I'm not interested in this idea that everybody is only an identity, and I'm definitely not interested in this idea that there are blank issues, like women's issues or black issues. If you are really good at hurting black people, you will indeed hurt the environment, I promise you.

[*applause*]

It's true.

[*applause*]

It's true. If you are really good at hurting women, you're probably also interested in war — I promise you. Do you understand what I mean?

[*applause*]

So I don't know why we think, in order to make narratives that somehow help us politically, we have to take people down to some kind of identity, as if that identity does not encapsulate the entirety of humanity and the entirety of humanity's needs. So when I say, "If you love me, you have to love me politically" — it's easy to know Jericho Brown, because "I'm cool. Hey, how you doin'" — but I have a history. I have an ancestry, and you gotta take all of that, when — if you're coming with me, that's what we're taking with us. And I'm going to take that part of you, as well. And I think, if we could just love each other a little more, whole, we all would be a lot better off. That's what I want my poems to point to.

TIPPETT: It makes me think of — I've sometimes interviewed — I've interviewed a lot of scientists. You talk to physicists and people who work with mathematics, and they say, "This thing we learn in school is" — I can see you're saying, "Where's she going with this?" [*laughs*] Yeah, OK. But, "This thing we learn in school is arithmetic. It's equations." And that's not — the people who work with mathematics, who are helping us understand the measure of the cosmos and help create all this technology we use...

BROWN: Yeah, exactly.

TIPPETT: ... They say, there's "mathematical thinking" that is so thrilling, that is such a thrilling part of the human enterprise. And that's not offered to us. And I kind of feel like what you're doing is "poetic thinking."

BROWN: Yes, I hope so.

TIPPETT: So it's not just a way of writing. It's a way of approaching something, like putting love and politics in the same sentence.

BROWN: Yes, yes, and being honest about those things. People keep looking for this pure poetry, and people have these questions about the political in poems, as if poems were ever not political. As far as I know, *The Iliad* and *The Odyssey* are about a war. And from that point on, poems ask us to find a place where we can absolutely rupture within ourselves. And I know nothing more political than asking yourself questions, asking yourself, "Am I right about that idea, or am I really messed up?" That's ultimately what it comes down to. And you have to take all of history and bring it down to one — one individual, one self — in order to do that.

TIPPETT: I'm Krista Tippett, and this is *On Being*. Today, with the poet Jericho Brown.

[*music: "Goodness" by Emancipator*]

TIPPETT: You were diagnosed with HIV, is that right?

BROWN: A thousand years ago.

TIPPETT: A thousand years ago.

BROWN: I'm still alive.

TIPPETT: I know, but you did write a poem about that, "To Be Seen."

BROWN: You want me to read it? You are asking me to read it. You were gonna ask me about it?

TIPPETT: Well, both. You can read it first, or talk about it first.

BROWN: I'll just read it. And then you can tell me. OK, let's see. This is exciting.

To Be Seen

"Forgive me for taking the tone of a preacher.
You understand, a dying man

Must have a point — not that I am
Dying exactly. My doctor tells me I'll live

Longer than most since I see him
More than most. Of course, he cannot be trusted

Nor can any man
Who promises you life for looking his way. Promises

Come from the chosen: a lunatic,
The whitest dove — those who hear

The voice of God and other old music. I'm not
Chosen. I only have a point like anyone

Paid to bring bad news: a preacher, a soldier,
The doctor. We talk about God

Because we want to speak
In metaphors. My doctor clings to the metaphor

Of war. It's always the virus
That attacks and the cells that fight or die

Fighting. Hell, I remember him saying the word
Siege when a rash returned. Here

I am dying while
He makes a battle of my body — anything to be seen

When all he really means is to grab me by the chin
And, like God the Father, say through clenched teeth,

Look at me when I'm talking to you.
Your healing is not in my hands, though

I touch as if to make you whole."

    [*applause*]

TIPPETT: You're just waiting for me to ask a question, aren't you.

BROWN: Yeah — well, yeah.

[*laughter*]

TIPPETT: What are you ...

BROWN: I'm realizing, for the first time in my life, that I've put things in books that I haven't read in front of people.

TIPPETT: You mean, right now, for the first time in your life, right here, with all of us as witnesses?

BROWN: There are things in books that — putting something in a book is very different from reading it in front of people. But I feel really good about this, though. It's really fascinating, to me, that very — the work you do when you're letting go and allowing whatever it is — like I think I said this earlier — you have to allow whatever wants to come, to come. The poems, the work you do has to have access to all of your life. So it's really interesting to talk about that in front of folk, to see that enacted in the last couple things I read.

TIPPETT: But that is the thing about writing, isn't it, because we can't — it's another part of us gets poured into that. We just don't walk around — we're not all in a Shakespeare play, speaking poetry to each other.

BROWN: It's part of the reason why — I think the most nervous I've been about this book that's called *The Tradition*. Get you some. But the book, in many ways, is about rape and sexual coercion and — which was, while I was writing it, what I knew I was supposed to be doing. And now that the book is coming out, there's not going to be any way for me to run from it when it's time to read those poems in front of people. So I'm preparing myself for that, because everybody enjoys their anonymity, but I understand that I've signed up for something that doesn't necessarily give me anonymity in the eyes of other people.

But I also understand, poems can only capture certain tones, and they're not how we feel about things forever. They're how we're capable of feeling about things when we write the poem. And I think writing poems, for me, helped transform my feeling about a lot of stuff. So I think this is really good practice, for me to read this stuff that you have me reading.

TIPPETT: Well, it's a pretty intense moment to be writing about rape and sexual violence, as well. Were you already writing about it, before it was …

BROWN: I had been writing it — my most recent book came out in 2014, and I realized that I had said a bunch of things, but that I hadn't told the entirety of the truth. I'd told part of the truth …

TIPPETT: About your parents?

BROWN: Well, actually, about HIV, and that I got HIV because I had been raped. So there's this book where I admit having HIV, because I realized, after my first book, I realized, you know what? You didn't say that. And you're thinking about that all the time, which means you're lying. You haven't given all of yourself. So you have to allow that, if that's what wants to come; you're going to have to allow it to come. And so, it came. It's not in every poem, but it's there.

And then this other book kept being about this thing, this idea that I have about Greek myth and about western civilization and about the murder of black bodies for absolutely no reason by police. And all of those things have to do — all of that encroaching is like a kind of rape. And in order for me to understand that kind of rape, I had to make it real and literal. So I had to use my own, which was really something I hadn't thought about, other than in therapists' chairs. Do you know what I mean? I really hadn't thought about how to make that into writing. So it was the hardest work I've ever done and yet the most inspired work.

And so now I'm in that stage, as the book — we're in galleys and doing the work we need to do to get the book bound. As we're doing that work, I'm thinking to myself, "Oh, this is so exciting; what the fuck have I done?" "Oh, my God, I can't wait till my book comes out — so that I can hide under my bed." Do you know what I mean? And I'll be fine; I read — actually, in New York a couple nights ago, and I got through it. I was crying and stuff, but I got through it.

So I'll just keep doing that, because ultimately, somebody needs it. I need to write those poems because I need to get to the next phase of my life, where I get over the stuff that I'm clearly holding in. That's what I need it for, and that's why I'm writing it first. But whenever I write a book, I find that there are people in the world who needed it. I'm not writing for that, but that's good to get.

TIPPETT: Well, that's that strange thing, that the more authentically and deeply we can speak from our particular experience, we speak to the particular experience of others.

BROWN: So true. It is so weird.

TIPPETT: It's not quite logical that it should work that way ...

BROWN: But it's true.

TIPPETT: ... but we say universal things, and they don't speak to the particular experience of others. Something you just said a minute ago, I just want to — I want to just underline that — that you are releasing this book in this moment where this whole matter of sexuality and rape and the spectrum of what leads to that is out in public; and my personal feeling is that we just scratched the surface. We reckon with it in public in these really imperfect, flawed situations. But what you just said about — that this reckoning with what happens to particular bodies, black bodies or women's bodies, is, actually — it's connected to this much larger civilizational reckoning with bodies.

BROWN: And what we've been told about them. Part of the reason why I say this is the hardest thing, and yet, the most inspiring thing — I think, in all my reading, I hadn't really been reading any poems that called rape, rape. We read a lot of poems where rape might happen, but we don't really realize that's what it is. Do you under-stand what I mean? I haven't read a lot of poems that really inter-rogate these questions about power and that really look at the fact that men still have no idea what rape is; that really look at — really, really will rape somebody and not know that they did it.

TIPPETT: Yeah.

BROWN: I'm interested in — if we're going to have these conversa-tions, I want to have them; and I have to have them in my genre. I think the conversations that are being had should be — if you're a preacher, you should have them in the pulpit. If you're an engineer, somehow you should — I don't care what you do. You should be having the conversation you're supposed to have.

TIPPETT: If you're a parent; if you're a teacher...

BROWN: And in spite of that, I think we're calling something, something, but we're not interrogating what it is, and we're not answering — like, what is the answer to sexual assault within a com-munity? We know what it is — what the answer is in the workplace. We know what the answer is in the law. What is the real answer in a community? And we have poetry communities where not-so-great things happen to women. So what do we do? What's our answer to that? And so I wanted to write poems that got at trying to figure that out for myself.

TIPPETT: What was something you said...

BROWN: Something I said.

TIPPETT: I don't know exactly —

BROWN: Everybody's like, what happened? We were having such a good time ...

[*laughter*]

[*music: "Voyages" by Thrupence*]

TIPPETT: After a short break, more with Jericho Brown. You can always listen again, and hear the unedited version of every show we do on the *On Being* podcast feed — wherever podcasts are found.

[*music: "Voyages" by Thrupence*]

TIPPETT: I'm Krista Tippett, and this is *On Being*. Today, experiencing the 2020 Pulitzer Prize winner for Poetry, the magnetic Jericho Brown. I was with him at the 2018 Geraldine R. Dodge Poetry Festival.

TIPPETT: Something you said about the similarity between poems and church services — that poems have structure, and they have music, and, you said, "and they even have surprises."

BROWN: Yeah — you don't know who's going to shout. I remember, I was in church one time — I think I was 10 or 11 years old, and I had just started wearing glasses. I couldn't see, the whole time I was growing up, and my mom and dad finally shelled out the money for me to get some glasses. This was huge in my family, by the way, because glasses were really — I remember they were like 100-and-something dollars. And anything that was three digits was not happening. I'm serious. Y'all think that's funny, but I'm serious. We were just blind. I didn't see a dentist until I was, like, 24 years old. Do you know what I mean? Anything that cost money, they were like, "How are we supposed to do that? We don't have money." And it was real.

So I had these glasses, and I was all excited because I could see. And this man next to me must've shouted so good and knocked my glasses clean across that church. I know. And they broke. And then — and you know how — you knew, going to church, somebody's going to get excited; but you didn't know when they were gonna get excited. You didn't know how it was going to manifest itself. And so, similarly, when I'm writing my poems, I'm thinking about structure in this way, and I'm trying to figure out, well, where is the surprise, for me? Where am I going to say the thing I don't expect to say?

TIPPETT: Right. I've had a similar conversation with Marilyn Nelson. I don't know if she's here in this room, but —

BROWN: She's great.

TIPPETT: She's wonderful. This whole thing about the structure and meaning and how they work together — I think you're saying this — you may be working with the structure or within the structure, and yet, you know the surprise can emerge from that and must emerge from that.

BROWN: Yeah, well, you haven't written anything until you say something you didn't expect to say. That's when you — and that's the beginning. You're sort of like, "Oh, here go some words. Oh, that's a nice word." Do you know what I mean? And then, suddenly — and you're looking, and as you're writing, you're making sentences, and suddenly you will say something that you have to hurry up and keep talking, because if you don't — you have to realize, "I just said something; that's crazy; and now I've got to keep going on that point. I can't run from that."

TIPPETT: Do you have an example, or a story, of what was happening in a poem surprising you? This could also be serious.

BROWN: I do. Actually, maybe I'll read one of the new poems.

TIPPETT: That'd be great.

BROWN: Is that OK with y'all?

[applause]

I'll read this one, because a lot of people saw it. It was in *Time* magazine. And it's the first time something really great happened to me, and I could tell my mom — because usually, good things happen — y'all know, I don't — my mother — I really don't think people who work at Kroger's, there's no expectation that you're going to bring your mom with you to go to work. And when you're an architect, and you design a building, there's no expectation that your mother's going to watch you draw the plans or walk through the building with you when it opens. Do y'all know what I mean? But when you're a poet, everybody's always like, "Well, did you send your book to your mother yet?"

TIPPETT: Right, right, right. [*laughs*]

BROWN: And I'm like, no; I ain't crazy.

[*laughter*]

What would I look like, sending my book to my mama? And so, we have an agreement.

TIPPETT: But this was in *Time* magazine? Is that what you said?

BROWN: Yeah, this poem was in *Time* magazine. I sent her the *Time* magazine. She was very happy.

TIPPETT: Yeah. That's good.

BROWN: She's like, "Oh, that was nice. Now you're finally writing nice poems."

[*laughter*]

I'm telling too much. Now y'all are gonna be like, "That wasn't nice."

Foreday in the Morning

My mother grew morning glories that spilled onto the walkway
     toward her porch
Because she was a woman with land who showed as much by giving
     it color.
She told me I could have whatever I worked for. That means she was
     an American.
But she'd say it was because she believed
In God. I am ashamed of America
And confounded by God. I thank God for my citizenship in spite
Of the timer set on my life to write
These words: I love my mother. I love black women
Who plant flowers as sheepish as their sons. By the time the blooms
Unfurl themselves for a few hours of light, the women who tend
     them
Are already at work. Blue. I'll never know who started the lie that
     we are lazy,
But I'd love to wake that bastard up
At foreday in the morning, toss him in a truck, and drive him under
     God
Past every bus stop in America to see all those black folk
Waiting to go work for whatever they want. A house? A boy
To keep the lawn cut? Some color in the yard? My God, we leave
     things green.

     [*applause*]

That's a poem. Thank you.

So literally, I got to say, "I love my mother" — which is a feeling I
actually have, and many of us have this feeling. But I've never had
any opportunity to say that. And it was the most emotional thing
for me, and it was a huge surprise to me, to get to a moment where

that was indeed the next thing. The thing the poem needed was a truth. And it seems a small truth. And yet, in that moment, it was the largest truth, because that love for my mother then becomes this love I have for an entire people in a way that — a sort of a way that I'm really bothered by — the way an entire people can be misunderstood.

So yeah, that's a surprise.

There are other surprises in this poem, like when I say, "I love black women / Who plant flowers as sheepish as their sons," which is me clearly talking about me when I was a kid, but also making that larger. So I like that. That's interesting. Surprises.

TIPPETT: Thank you. That's fun, for you to share that with us.

BROWN: I think my way of making a poem is very different from other people's way of making a poem. I do this in several ways. One of the ways I do it is, I have a bunch of things that didn't work, and I just put them together and they're all on different pages and I cut them up, and I set them on a table, and it's like I'm putting a puzzle together. But what I do other than that is I write a line, and then I write another line because it riffs off of the sound of that line, and I keep doing that, thinking about the rhythm and the sounds of the line before the line, but not thinking about what I'm saying. So sometimes, I'll have notation; I'll know that a sound needs to be there, and that sound might be a word, like "road," but the sentence won't make — the line won't make any sense as we think about sense. But I don't care that it doesn't make any sense. I write the next line after that, which sounds something like that line. And then, once I've done that, I hit something that makes me — where I feel spent. And I look at that mess of words, and I start asking it questions. And this is how I'm better able to get at the subconscious, because I have the experience that I have when we're looking at a painting. When we look at a painting, a painting is —

TIPPETT: Yeah, it's kind of impressionistic, but with words.

BROWN: It doesn't matter how concrete or abstract the painting is, something in us is driven to say, "This is about..." We'll give it a beginning, a present, and we'll give it an after. We see two people talking across the lawn, across a campus or something. There's something in us that wants to imagine what they're talking about. "Oh, he's getting it now. I knew she wasn't going to put up with that." You don't know them people.

TIPPETT: Yeah, and what are they to each other; what's their relationship...

BROWN: Exactly. And if you ask the poem questions, things you think, things that you have experienced, things you live will begin to come out.

TIPPETT: Your process is structured to yield surprise.

BROWN: Exactly. Exactly. Just ask it questions, and you'll find out what you've really been thinking. So what I'm saying is, we bring to language whatever we're already thinking about, and our job is to really find out, to dig, and see, "What do I really think? What am I really —" — that's what I'm trying to do while I'm writing.

TIPPETT: And that interrogation is not always happening. That is true in every moment; we're all bringing something to what we see and how we feel about it and how we interpret it. But this is the process of taking that on, taking that in.

BROWN: Yes. What is it that you're bringing — that's a very good way — what do you bring to the moment that you're not aware you're bringing to the moment? And if you can figure that out, then you can also become more of who you indeed are, because you're facing what you really think, who you really are. And you can make

99

a decision like, "Do I want to be that person, or do I want to more fully inhabit and become this person I have been being?"

TIPPETT: I'm Krista Tippett, and this is *On Being*. Today, with the poet, Jericho Brown.

[*music: "Train View" by Niklas Aman*]

TIPPETT: I think, unfortunately, we have to wind down, but —

BROWN: Oh, that's too bad.

TIPPETT: I know. See? I said, we could just keep nattering up here.

BROWN: Well, you know, we laughed, we cried.

TIPPETT: We did. [*laughs*]

In the credo — so one thing I feel about the world right now is, there's a scarcity — there's a fragility to hope right now. I experience a lot of people saying, it's hard to know that what you do, what I do, can make a difference, although it feels like there's so much we want to change. I want to read something you wrote in that credo. You said, "Hope is always accompanied by the imagination, the will to see what our physical environment seems to deem impossible. Only the creative mind can make use of hope. Only a creative people can wield it."

BROWN: Come on. Come on!

TIPPETT: Do you like having your words read back to you?

BROWN: Say that again. That was good. Y'all heard that?

[*laughter*]

Now, that's the Dodge anthem right there. I like that. That was good. I write that?

TIPPETT: You did, yeah.

BROWN: Clap that, all right. Y'all know that was good. Say that again.

[*applause*]

TIPPETT: I'm going to.

BROWN: That's very good. Y'all listen. Y'all write it down. Oh, it's online. I think it's online. You can get some of the words and Google it.

TIPPETT: "Hope is always accompanied by the imagination, the will to see what our physical environment seems to deem impossible. Only the creative mind can make use of hope. Only a creative people can wield it."

BROWN: Come on, creative people. I got some creative people out there, yes, God.

[*applause*]

Y'all better go hope. I like that. Oh, my God. I be writing.

TIPPETT: There's something else — this goes together with that. I love this.

BROWN: People should pay me way more.

[*laughter*]

I'm serious.

TIPPETT: They should [*laughs*] So here's the other thing. It's like people feel right now like it's hard not to be captive to the loud voices, the loud stories, the bad stories, the catastrophes.

BROWN: Yeah; oh, my God.

TIPPETT: And also, what there is to — there's a lot to worry about. You said this — "An event happening ten minutes or ten years ago matters if anyone can indeed feel the effects of it now." That feels really important to me too, because — anyone. If you have something you did ten minutes ago, one person feels the effect of it, that's a metric.

BROWN: Yeah, I agree. This isn't a question. You just want me to say something about that?

TIPPETT: [*laughs*] I'm just using the occasion of having you sitting across from me to affirm what you said.

BROWN: I agree. We're taught — I don't know. I've been asking my friends this lately a lot; why are we doing all of this? Somebody introduced me as a "cultural worker," and I feel like that, and I'm sort of like, but why am I doing all that? And then I realized that it was in the title — that what I do, I do for culture; that I create culture; that I live in and benefit from culture, and that art and that culture make my life worth living and that it pushes me on to see more art, to make more things; that I'm a person who believes in living as one would want to see a life; that I really do believe in making the poems that I want to be in the world, in teaching the classes that I would want to see if I were a student, in dancing the way I like to see people dance. Do you know what I mean?

And I think, for me, knowing that I can do that is what I have. And I'm hoping that for more people, that can be what you have in this moment; that instead of looking at the things that mean to hurt us, that we can look at each other; that we can hold up in the opposite direction some poetry; that we can hold up in the opposite direction some song; that we can hold up in the opposite direction some belief we have in some community project, some play, something that we are doing, some child that we love; and that I think if we can concentrate on the best of one another, on the best of the best of us, if we can really make the world we want to live in — even if it's only in our own heads or in our own homes or in our own cars on the way to work — then we'll be doing the beginning of something new.

[*applause*]

TIPPETT: I feel like we should end with a poem.

BROWN: Hey. And thank y'all so much …

TIPPETT: Oh, it's page 54.

BROWN: … for being here. I appreciate it.

[*applause*]

Psalm 150

Some folks fool themselves into believing,
But I know what I know once, at the height
Of hopeless touching, my man and I hold
Our breaths, certain we can stop time or maybe

Eliminate it from our lives, which are shorter
Since we learned to make love for each other
Rather than doing it to each other. As for praise
And worship, I prefer the latter. Only memory

Makes us kneel, silent and still. Hear me?
Thunder scares. Lightning lets us see. Then,
Heads covered, we wait for rain. Dear Lord,
Let me watch for his arrival and hang my head

And shake it like a man who's lost and lived.
Something keeps trying, but I'm not killed yet."

Thank you.

[*applause*]

TIPPETT: Thank you. Thank you.

[*music: "Feel Good (Instrumental)" by Broke For Free*]

TIPPETT: Jericho Brown is Winship Research Professor in Creative Writing at Emory University in Atlanta. He also directs the university's creative writing program. His books of poetry are *The New Testament*, *Please*, and *The Tradition*, for which he won the 2020 Pulitzer Prize.

The On Being Project is located on Dakota Land. Our lovely theme music is provided and composed by Zoë Keating. And the last voice that you hear singing at the end of our show is Cameron Kinghorn.

On Being is an independent, nonprofit production of the On Being Project. It's distributed to public radio stations by WNYC Studios. I created this show at American Public Media.

COMMUNITY CONNECTION

Reach Out to Us

ADDITIONAL RESOURCES:

Civil Conversations Project: http://bit.ly/onbeing-ccp
Grounding Virtues: http://bit.ly/onbeing-virtues
Better Conversations Guide: http://bit.ly/onbeing-guide
One Book, One Philadelphia: *The Tradition* Discussion Guide:
https://libwww.freelibrary.org/programs/onebook/obop21/
docs/one-book-discussion-guide-the-tradition.pdf

Some *On Being* Episodes We Recommend

Resmaa Menakem: *Notice the Rage; Notice the Silence*
Robin DiAngelo and Resmaa Menakem: *Towards a Framework
    for Repair*
Frances Kissling: *What Is Good in the Position of the Other*
Ruby Sales: *Where Does It Hurt?*
John Lewis: *Love in Action*
Ross Gay: *Tending Joy and Practicing Delight*
Pádraig Ó Tuama: *Belonging Creates and Undoes Us*
Jason Reynolds: *Imagination and Fortitude*
Brené Brown: *Strong Back, Soft Front, Wild Heart*
Isabel Wilkerson: *This History Is Long: This History Is Deep*
Ocean Vuong: *A Life Worthy of Our Breath*
Eula Biss: *Talking About Whiteness*
Derek Black and Matthew Stevenson: *Befriending Radical
    Disagreement*
America Ferrera and John Paul Lederach: *The Ingredients of
    Social Change*
Rebecca Solnit: *Falling Together*
Sharon Salzberg and Robert Thurman: *Love Your Enemies?
    (Really?)*

ABOUT THE AUTHOR

Jericho Brown is the recipient of a Whiting Award and of fellowships from the John Simon Guggenheim Foundation, the Radcliffe Institute for Advanced Study at Harvard University, and the National Endowment for the Arts. His poems have appeared in *Fence, jubilat, The New Criterion, The New Republic, The New Yorker, The New York Times, Time,* and several of *The Best American Poetry* anthologies. His first book, *Please* (New Issues, 2008), won the American Book Award. His second book, *The New Testament* (Copper Canyon, 2014), won the Anisfield-Wolf Book Award. He serves as poetry editor for *The Believer.* He is an associate professor of English and Creative Writing and Director of the Creative Writing Program at Emory University in Atlanta.

Poetry is vital to language and living. Since 1972, Copper Canyon Press has published extraordinary poetry from around the world to engage the imaginations and intellects of readers, writers, booksellers, librarians, teachers, students, and donors.

COPPER CANYON PRESS WISHES TO EXTEND A SPECIAL THANKS TO THE FOLLOWING SUPPORTERS WHO PROVIDED FUNDING DURING THE COVID-19 PANDEMIC:

4Culture
Academy of American Poets (Literary Relief Fund)
City of Seattle Office of Arts & Culture
Community of Literary Magazines and Presses (Literary Relief Fund)
Economic Development Council of Jefferson County
National Book Foundation (Literary Relief Fund)
Poetry Foundation
U.S. Department of the Treasury Payroll Protection Program

WE ARE GRATEFUL FOR THE MAJOR SUPPORT

PROVIDED BY:

TO LEARN MORE ABOUT UNDERWRITING
COPPER CANYON PRESS TITLES,
PLEASE CALL 360-385-4925 EXT. 103

WE ARE GRATEFUL FOR THE MAJOR SUPPORT
PROVIDED BY:

Richard Andrews
Anonymous (3)
Jill Baker and Jeffrey Bishop
Anne and Geoffrey Barker
In honor of Ida Bauer, Betsy
    Gifford, and Beverly Sachar
Donna Bellew
Matthew Bellew
Sarah Bird
Will Blythe
John Branch
Diana Broze
John R. Cahill
Sarah Cavanaugh
Stephanie Ellis-Smith and
    Douglas Smith
Austin Evans
Saramel Evans
Mimi Gardner Gates
Gull Industries Inc. on behalf of
    William True
The Trust of Warren A. Gummow
William R. Hearst III
Carolyn and Robert Hedin
David and Jane Hibbard
Bruce Kahn
Phil Kovacevich and Eric Wechsler

Lakeside Industries Inc. on behalf
    of Jeanne Marie Lee
Maureen Lee and Mark Busto
Peter Lewis and Johnna Turiano
Ellie Mathews and Carl Youngmann
    as The North Press
Larry Mawby and Lois Bahle
Hank and Liesel Meijer
Jack Nicholson
Gregg Orr
Petunia Charitable Fund and
    adviser Elizabeth Hebert
Suzanne Rapp and Mark Hamilton
Adam and Lynn Rauch
Emily and Dan Raymond
Joseph C. Roberts
Jill and Bill Ruckelshaus
Cynthia Sears
Kim and Jeff Seely
Joan F. Woods
Barbara and Charles Wright
In honor of C.D. Wright,
    from Forrest Gander
Caleb Young as C. Young Creative
The dedicated interns and
    faithful volunteers of
    Copper Canyon Press

The book you are holding is a testament to the diverse community of passionate readers who supported "Jericho Brown's *The Tradition: Civic Dialogue Edition*." Copper Canyon Press is deeply grateful to the following individuals around the world whose philanthropic vision and love of poetry made this legacy collection possible. We have published *The Tradition, Civic Dialogue Edition* together. Thank you!

Nancy and Craig Abramson

Elissa Altman

Melissa Anderson

Virginia Anderson

Karin Lisa Atkinson

Claudia J. Bach

Andrew Bartel

Baycafewriter

David Alexander Beame

Opal and Louise Bednarik

Dana Bettinger

Dicken Bettinger

Sarah Bird

Twanna P. Bolling

Marianne Botos

Joan M. Broughton

Dori Celia Cahn

Lisa J.A. Charnock

In Memory of Mrs.
    Catherine M. Clem

Katharine Weston Cohen

Elizabeth J. Coleman

Hannah Crawforth

Dave Davis

In memory of Melvin Dixon

Maureen E. Doallas

Catherine Edwards

In memory of Manuel Ellis

Katrina Ernst

Nancy Fowler

Jerome Gentes and
    Michael Bourque

Linda Gerrard

Lizzie Giglio

Kristy Gledhill

Yolanda Graham, M.D. and
    Tiffany Courtney

In memory of Bry Green

Valerie Griffith

Laura P. Grissom

Gunner Hancock

Dr. Telaireus K. Herrin

Simon Højberg

Clifford Hume

Bertram Johnson

Sarah Heath Johnson

Kenneth Jones

Patrick Gage Kelley

Claire Keyes

M. E. Keyes

Stephen V. Kobasa

Krzycho & Rauni

Jennifer Markell

Kara and Ken Masters

In memory of Pellom
    McDaniels III

Sandra Meek

Megan

Trey Moody

Elizabeth Douglas Mornin

Vincent O. Odamtten

Kathy O'Driscoll

Ronald Olufunwa

Cara Parrish

Mickey Pearson

Persephone Farm

Justin Peters

Oona & Silas Petrosky

Randy Pottebaum

R~

Geila Rajaee

Emily Raymond

Sara and Tripp Ritter

Joseph Roberts

Linda M. Robertson

Robert Rolston

Tristan Destry Saldaña

Pamela Jean Sampel

Mike Sanders

Paul Santiago

Lauret Edith Savoy

Nobunari Sawanobori

The Steere Family

In memory of Rabbi
    Sarah Tauber

LaKara M. Ticeson

Maria Van Newkirk

Rolland Vasin aka Vachine

Margaret H. Wagner

Moira Walsh

Whale Road Review

Shangrila Willy

Trina Woldt & Richard Lanzetta

Jay Yencich

The Chinese character for poetry is made up of two parts:
"word" and "temple." It also serves as pressmark for
Copper Canyon Press.

The poems are set Fournier.
Book design and composition by Phil Kovacevich.

CPSIA information can be obtained
at www.ICGtesting.com
Printed in the USA
JSHW030058220322
R11516400001B/R115164PG24075JSX00001B/1